Editor
Eric Migliaccio

Managing Editor
Ina Massler Levin, M.A.

Illustrator
Mark Mason

Cover Artist
Denise Bauer

Art Manager
Kevin Barnes

Art Director
CJae Froshay

Imaging
Rosa C. See

All Artwork @Mary Engelbreit Ink
www.maryengelbreit.com

Publisher
Mary D. Smith, M.S. Ed.

Dayton

W9-BYA-949

Author

Melissa Hart, M.F.A.

Teacher Created Resources, Inc.
6421 Industry Way
Westminster, CA 92683
www.teachercreated.com
ISBN-1-4206-3138-1
©2005 Teacher Created Resources, Inc.
Made in U.S.A.

Table of Contents

Table of Contents *(cont.)*

Introduction

A love of reading can broaden a child's perspective, inspiring creativity and passion. Books can teach, entertain, and motivate children to strive toward exhilarating goals. By using a variety of innovative approaches, *101 Ways to Love a Book* is designed to help teachers and parents give the gift of reading to children. Each activity allows readers to deepen their understanding of, and appreciation for, a favorite book.

Children learn well when offered activities that cater to individual learning styles across the curriculum. With this in mind, *101 Ways to Love a Book* presents a multitude of suggestions for the following:

* Arts and Crafts
* Recreational Games
* Creative Writing
* Oral Reports
* Classroom Debate
* Community-based Activities
* Film and Photography
* Graphic Design
* Audio Recording
* Peer Tutoring
* Gardening
* Science Projects
* Theater Activities

Some activities are designed for individuals or small groups to complete independently. Others are teacher-directed, and some are designed to be completed school-wide. Look on the bottom of each page for a coded label that shows for whom the activity will be the most appropriate. Here is a quick reference guide to the codes used in this book:

IN = Individual Activity

GR = Group Activity

TD = Teacher-Directed Activity

SW = School-wide Activity

One of the most influential actions you can take to foster a love of reading in a child is to share your enthusiasm for books. As you work through the activities in *101 Ways to Love a Book*, discuss your own favorite books with your students. Allowing children to observe your pleasure in reading books will inspire them to enjoy reading. Perhaps they will then pass on a love of books to someone else!

1

Make a Diorama

A diorama is a three-dimensional scene set against a decorated background. Choose a favorite scene from your book to depict in your diorama. Then gather together a shoebox with a lid, scissors, and glue. You may choose to use crayons, paints, pastels, colored pencils, or markers. For the ground of your diorama, use sand, dirt, straw, grass, rocks, leaves, carpet, or felt.

First, sketch the scene you wish to create. What characters will you depict? Think about what is on the ground in this scene. Ask yourself, what is in the background? Are there interesting objects such as trees or buildings or animals in this scene?

Now, remove the lid from your shoebox and trace characters and objects on the lid. Cut them out and color them appropriately. Make a stand so that your characters can stand upright.

Place the shoebox on one side. Inside, on the back of the box, draw or paint background scenery. Perhaps your characters are in a park or in the city? Maybe they're in a kitchen or driving along a road? You may choose to cut out objects and paste them inside, on the back of your shoebox.

Now, glue appropriate ground covering on one side of the box. This may be sand, dirt, straw, grass, etc.

Finally, position your characters inside the box with any objects that you feel would be appropriate.

Display this diorama of your favorite scene for others to enjoy!

IN/GR

Show and Tell

Think about the themes in your book. How can you explore them further by sharing knowledge with classmates, friends, or family?

Does your book have to do with rabbits? Perhaps you could bring a pet rabbit to class one day and share everything you know about rabbit behavior.

Maybe one of the themes in your book involves a garden. Why not share seeds, soil, and small pots made out of the cardboard sections of egg cartons as you teach people how to plant flowers or vegetables?

Does your book focus on the importance of music? Share your favorite songs on tape or CD, or play an instrument to help others appreciate music.

Have fun exploring your book's theme, showing and telling all that you've learned with other people!

GR

3

Dress-Up Party

Host a dress-up party in honor of your book. Invite your friends and family to celebrate with you in costume.

You'll need colored paper and pens or pencils for the invitations, costumes, and food and drinks.

First, decide what day and time your party will take place. Then, make invitations and send them two weeks before the party. Let people know that they should come dressed as a character from one of their favorite books or from a book that you have selected.

Now, decide what food and drink you will serve at your party. Perhaps the menu will be related to your book in some way. You may choose to serve tea and scones for a book about the English aristocracy, baked beans and s'mores for a book set in the outdoors, or vegetables fresh from the garden for a book in which the main characters are animals.

Decide on what character you will portray. A parent's or grandparent's old clothes or clothing from a thrift store can make a wonderful costume. Think about how your character would dress, and gather the items you need. Don't forget accessories, such as hats, jewelry, and makeup.

A day before the party, make food and drinks. Try on your costume to spot any last-minute adjustments. On the day of the party, thank people for coming. Ask each guest to stand briefly and describe his or her character and costume. Have a good time!

GR

Wanted Posters

The police use wanted posters to help them locate criminals. You can find these posters in the post office, in the courthouse, and, of course, in the police station.

Using heavy white paper and black markers, create "Wanted" posters for the characters in your novel. Draw a picture of each character, and write an accurate description of that character below the picture.

You should include the following information:

- age
- height
- weight
- build
- hair color
- eye color
- race and/or nationality
- hairstyle
- clothing your character was last seen wearing

For an example of a wanted poster, type the words "wanted poster" into your favorite Internet search engine.

5

Choreograph a Dance

Some of the most famous stories have been turned into ballets and other dances. *Sleeping Beauty, Romeo and Juliet,* and *Beauty and the Beast* are among the classics.

With time and imagination, you, too, can choreograph a dance in celebration of a favorite book.

First, choose your music. It may be classical, rock, hip-hop—the choice is yours!

Now, figure out how to tell your story through dance. Will you need more than one dancer? Choreograph moves with the help of others. Practice with your chosen music until you have your dance just right.

Think about costumes. What types of clothing will your dancers wear to give an impression of the book's characters and plot? For further ideas on costuming, research dance on the Internet and in books and encyclopedias.

Now, consider giving a live performance. Invite people to watch you dance. You might want to explain a little about your book before the performance. Also, you may wish to follow the dance by answering any questions your audience might have about the characters, conflict, and resolution.

An alternative to live performance is to videotape your dance. That way, you can watch yourself perform!

IN/GR

Write a Sequel

What happens to the characters in your book after you finish reading the final page? Why not create a sequel? A *sequel* is a book that is published after the first book has enjoyed success among readers. For example, the sequel to Madeleine L'Engle's novel *A Wrinkle in Time is A Wind in the Door.* A sequel picks up where the first book left off.

To begin a sequel to your favorite book, first think about how the original story ends. What adventures might the characters have next? How do they continue to grow and change?

Now, write a rough draft of your sequel. Edit for grammar, punctuation, and spelling. Come up with a compelling title.

Finally, write or type the final draft of your sequel on clean paper. Consider illustrating your book. You may choose to write your sequel in a notebook or bind your pages using a variety of methods.

Whatever you choose, your sequel is sure to provide exciting reading for others who have finished the same book and wondered, "What happens next?"

IN/GR

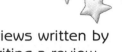

7

Write a Book Review

Did you know that many online and print magazines run book reviews written by young people? If you love a particular book, why not consider writing a review about it?

First, explain why you liked the book. Tell a little about it—but don't give away the entire plot. If there's a mystery involved, avoid solving it. Just give readers a sense of why the book is good and why they should read it.

Add anything else you feel is important about the book, such as how it made you feel and what you learned from it.

Now, type up your review. Check your grammar, punctuation, and spelling. When everything looks correct, either print your review out or paste it into the body of an e-mail. Write a brief letter to the magazine editor, and tell him or her a little about yourself. Include your age, grade, address, and phone number.

Finally, send your book review to the magazine. You may choose to investigate one of the magazines below, or submit your review to one of your own favorite publications.

Online Reviews

- *http://www.worldreading.org*
- *http://www.spaghettibookclub.org*
- *http://www.buildingrainbows.com*
- *http://cuip.uchicago.edu/~nvolkman/forms/reviewform.htm*

Print Magazine Reviews

- *Creative Kids*
- *Skipping Stones*
- *Stone Soup*
- *Potluck Children's Literary Magazine*
- *The Writer's Slate*

IN

Make a Bookworm

Teacher Note: For this activity, supply each student with a 6" circle cut from construction paper. Use different colors of paper so that the final product is as colorful as possible. On one circle of paper, draw a face. This will be the head of the bookworm.

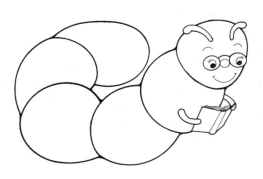

For this activity, your teacher will give you one circle of construction paper. On that circle, write the name of your book, the name of the author, and a brief description of the book. You may also want to decorate your circle appropriately with markers, stickers, glitter, etc.

On the bulletin board, your teacher will staple a circle that has a face on it. When everyone in the class has completed their circles, staple them behind the face circle to make a classroom bookworm.

You can do this project at home, too! Just complete one circle of your bookworm for every book you read. As you complete a circle, tack it to your wall. Don't forget to make a face circle to put in front of the others. Read as many books as possible, and see how long you can get your bookworm to grow!

IN/GR

12

Make a Movie

Many books have been made into wonderful movies. Some examples include *The Lord of the Rings* trilogy; *Ella Enchanted; Sarah, Plain and Tall; Anne of Green Gables;* and *The Adventures of Huckleberry Finn.* You can make your own movie based on your favorite book. All you need is a video camera and a blank tape!

First, write a script for your movie. You may choose to film only one scene, or perhaps you'll act out the whole story! Decide how many actors you'll need.

Now, think about costumes. What will each actor wear to look authentic in his or her role?

Think about setting. Where will you film your movie? Is it most accurate to film it in a house, a garage, a barn, or outdoors?

Rehearse your script until people feel comfortable performing in front of a video camera. You may borrow a video camera from your parents or friends, from your school, or rent one from a local camera store.

Now, film your movie. If you are one of the actors, you may ask someone else to film it for you, or you may wish to mount the video camera on a tripod.

When you are finished with your movie, pop some popcorn and host a film screening!

GR

Volunteer

Get to know your characters and their situations better by volunteering for a local cause related to your book. Perhaps the main character in your story loves dogs. Why not volunteer for an afternoon at the local animal shelter? Maybe one character has a younger brother, but you're an only child. You can volunteer to work with children at the Boys' and Girls' Club or at a daycare facility for an afternoon.

Here are some other ideas for places to volunteer:

❣ Water trees and flowers at a plant nursery.

❣ Feed and pet the animals at a pet store.

❣ Pick fruit or flowers on a farm.

❣ Make breakfast for people at a homeless shelter.

❣ Clean stalls at a horse stable.

❣ Plant seeds and pull weeds at a community garden.

❣ Pick up trash at a park or local beach.

❣ Have a conversation with someone in a retirement home.

❣ Clean cages at a local zoo or raptor center.

❣ Teach children a new skill during recess or at an after-school program.

When you are finished volunteering, give an oral or written report about your experience.

IN/GR/TD

11

Read-Together Charts

Does your father read books to you before bed? Perhaps your mother reads to the family at breakfast? Your grandparents may enjoy reading books to you after school or on the weekends. You and your family members can create a Read-Together Chart and fill it in to keep track of all the books you've read together.

Here is a sample of a Read-Together Chart. You may choose to model your chart on this sample, or create your own!

Sample Chart

Book We Read	Who Read It?	Description	Our Review
The Secret Garden	My older sister read it to me.	It's about a spoiled girl who learns to love nature and people.	We love this book. The characters are funny, and the illustrations are beautiful!

IN

Go to a Museum

Whether your favorite book is historical, scientific, artistic, or otherwise, you can learn more about your characters and their world by visiting a museum.

Maybe your character likes art. Why not visit a local art museum and take along a blank notebook? Pretend to be your favorite character, taking notes and making sketches of all that you observe. Don't forget to visit the gift shop. Which postcard would your character be most likely to purchase?

Perhaps your character loves nature. The natural history museum is a wonderful place to learn more about insects, trees, flowers, plants, amphibians, fish, reptiles, and mammals. You may also learn about the local history of your area. Approach the museum from your character's point of view. Record interesting facts in a notebook, along with your impressions. Add drawings to illustrate your observations.

Your character may love science. Many cities have a science museum. Is your character interested in one particular aspect of science, such as space travel or electricity? Investigate this subject in depth, and then write up a scientific report from the point of view of your character.

Some cities offer specialty museums. Look for museums with exhibits on dolls, toys, neon, animation, health, geology, Native Americans, birds, marine life, quilts—the list goes on and on!

IN/GR/TD

13

Make a Mobile

A mobile consists of a suspended crosspiece and several items or pictures that hang off of that crosspiece. You can make a mobile to hang from your ceiling, in order to illustrate your book.

You'll need cardboard or colored paper; scissors; a hole-punch; yarn; two wooden craft sticks; and drawing implements, such as crayons, colored pencils, markers, and/or paint. You'll also need thumbtacks, a stapler, or tape to affix your mobile to the ceiling.

Begin by drawing four pictures of important characters and/or scenes from your book on cardboard or colored paper. Color your pictures, then cut them out. Punch one hole in the top of each picture. Thread a foot-long piece of yarn through the hole in each picture and tie the yarn securely, leaving about 10 inches of yarn free to hang from the crosspiece.

Now, make the crosspiece for your mobile. Using a foot-long piece of yarn, bind the two craft sticks together firmly in the shape of an X. Leave three inches of yarn to affix to the ceiling.

Tie your pictures to the four ends of the crosspiece so that they hang down. Finally, affix your mobile to the ceiling with a thumbtack, staple, or tape.

IN/GR

Design a Travel Brochure

Cities often offer a travel brochure—a tri-folded piece of paper featuring pictures and text designed to get people interested in coming to visit. Where does your character live? In the city? In the country? In a fantasy world? What do you imagine would attract tourists to this place?

Create a travel brochure designed to tell people all about your book's setting. (For an example of a travel brochure, call your local Chamber of Commerce and ask them to send you one.) You'll need two pieces of paper (8 ½" x 11"); crayons, markers, or colored pencils; scissors; glue; rub-on letters; and old photographs or old magazines.

Fold your first piece of paper into thirds. This will be the rough draft. On this piece of paper, sketch a design for your travel brochure. Include space for pictures, as well as plenty of room for writing.

When you have completed your rough draft, fold your other piece of paper into thirds. This will be the final draft. Cut out and glue pictures in designated places. Write text above and/or below the pictures. You might choose to use rub-on letters for an especially professional-looking brochure.

When you are finished with your brochure, display it alongside your book.

IN/GR

15

Design a Bookmark

These days, book publishers often create bookmarks to help promote a particular book. You can design a bookmark for your favorite book. You'll need a strip of heavy paper (4" x 8"). Include the following information on your bookmark:

❣ title of the book

❣ author

❣ publisher

❣ price

❣ a brief description of the book

❣ a picture of the book's cover

❣ a quote by you, explaining why people should read this book

> Adventures In Africa
>
> by Joan Meyers
> ATC Publishers
>
> A story about growing up in Africa
>
> AFRICA
>
> This is an exciting book for all to read!

Consider punching a hole in the top of your bookmark and threading two pieces of colorful yarn through it, knotting the ends into a tassel.

Once you have completed your bookmark, you may want to laminate it with plastic. Your teacher may be able to do this, or you may take your bookmark to a copy shop for lamination.

IN

Record an Old-Time Radio Show

In the days before television, people listened to stories on the radio. Detective stories like *The Adventures of Sherlock Homes* and comedies like *The Burns and Allen Show* had people crowding around the radio every evening.

You can turn your favorite book into an old-time radio show. All you need is a tape recorder, some willing actors, and props to create exciting sound effects.

First, write a script for a particular scene or for the entire book. Assign actors their parts. You may want to photocopy the script and give a copy to each of your actors. Discuss sound effects. In the past, radio producers used bells, whistles, kazoos, horns, and even old shoes clomping on the ground in order to bring their stories to life. What will you use to create intriguing sound effects?

Finally, record your radio show. Make sure to have an announcer who will read the title of your show and introduce the actors. Speak slowly and clearly, remembering to add emotion as you talk. You may want to pause halfway through your script—as old-time radio actors did—to do a commercial for a favorite product. Then, return to your story.

When you have finished recording your radio show, play it for friends, family, and your classmates.

GR

17

Character Report Cards

You have most likely received report cards from your school detailing your past accomplishments and your goals for the future. Now it's your turn to act as the teacher. Think about the characters in your book. What are their strong points? How could they improve? Perhaps a character is a really fast runner, but she's afraid to compete in a race. She might want to focus on taking on new challenges. Another character may love horses and work well with them, but he gets into fights with kids at school. His goal may be anger management.

Fill out a report-card form like the one below for as many characters in your book as you can. Evaluate each character's behavior, and add comments at the bottom of the chart, such as outstanding achievements, suggestions for improvement, and other important observations. You may want to discuss these report cards with other people who have read your book.

Character's Name: _____

Character's Strong Points: _____

Goals for Future: _____

	Behavior	Beginning Grade	Ending Grade
Kind Polite Mature Generous Smart Helpful			
Comments:			

IN

Write to the Author

Many authors love to get letters from their readers, telling them what people liked best about their books. You can write to an author and send your letter in care of the book's publisher. The publisher's address is listed directly after the title page. (To make sure your author is still living, do a search on the Internet, typing your author's name into a search engine.)

First, write a rough draft of your letter. What do you want to say to the author? You might mention characters or scenes you liked best in the book. Maybe you want to describe what you learned from the book or how it changed you. Feel free to tell the author a little about yourself, as well. Include such information as your age, grade, and interests.

Now, copy your letter on nice paper. You may want to decorate it with drawings or stickers. Perhaps you'll enclose a picture of yourself, as well. Make sure to put your name and address at the top of your letter so that the author can write back to you if he or she wishes.

Finally, fold your letter and put it in an envelope. Write your return address in the top left corner. In the middle of the envelope, write the author's name. Below that, write "care of" and then the publisher's name and address.

Don't forget to affix a first-class stamp before you mail your letter. In a few weeks or months, you may be surprised to receive a letter back from your favorite author!

IN

19

Host a Story Hour

Why not share your favorite book with another class? Meet up with students from a younger grade for an afternoon of reading. You may choose to go to another classroom, or younger students may come to your classroom.

First, choose a favorite book that is appropriate for a younger student. Practice reading out loud. You should read slowly and clearly, in a voice loud enough to be heard but quiet enough to allow other students in the room to listen to their own readers. You may choose to read in different voices for different characters.

When you have finished practicing, pair up with a younger student. Listen as he or she reads a favorite book. Then read your favorite book, or part of it, to the student. Compare notes about what you liked best about both books. Talk about what books you want to read in the future. Perhaps you'll want to make plans to read together again!

GR/TD/SW

Tour Your Public Library

The public library is a treasure chest of books, magazines, music, books on tape, newspapers, and more! With your teacher or your family, visit your public library. You may want to call in advance and arrange a tour with a librarian. Or, you can use the questions below for a self-guided tour of your local library.

1. Where is the children's section of the library?

2. What kinds of magazines can I read at the library?

3. Does my library offer books on tape?

4. What kind of music does my library offer?

5. Where are the newspapers located in my library?

6. Where can I find encyclopedias and atlases?

7. Does my library offer free Internet access?

8. What are the rules for reading and studying in my library?

9. How can I get a library card?

10. How many books am I allowed to check out at once?

IN/GR/TD

Accordion Books

Accordion books are a fun way to illustrate your book's plot. First, identify the introduction, rising action, climax, falling action, and conclusion in your book. Figure out which five scenes in the book best illustrate these plot elements. Then, create your accordion book.

You'll need six pieces of cardboard; tape; and markers, colored pencils, crayons, or paint.

Cut six pieces of cardboard that are the same size and shape. They don't have to be rectangles: feel free to experiment with different shapes. Then, tape the six pieces of cardboard together at the sides. (See the illustration to the right.) Now, draw the cover for your accordion book, on the piece of cardboard to the far left. Then, draw the five scenes that illustrate your book's introduction, rising action, climax, falling action, and conclusion.

Write a brief synopsis of each scene on the appropriate book page.

You can add excitement to your pages with glitter, stickers, rubber stamps, and sequins. Display your book for others to read and enjoy.

IN/GR

Book Freeze!

Over the course of a month, each student is allowed to read or recite a paragraph from a favorite book. Students can choose the time and day of their reading. This can be a fun assignment, especially when a student leaps up in the middle of a test and calls, "Freeze!" and then reads his or her paragraph.

What paragraph will you read, and when will you read it? During math class? On a field trip? The choice is up to you!

GR/TD

23

Book Bingo

On a piece of paper, list 25 book titles, characters' names, or details from a single book.

Make up bingo cards on squares of cardboard, with five columns and five rows. In each square, write a title, name, or book detail. Arrange these differently on every bingo card.

Using pennies or dried beans as playing pieces, begin to play. One person is the "caller," and he or she calls out a title, name, or detail about the book. Players mark the appropriate square on their cards with a penny or bean. The first person to mark five squares up, down, or diagonally wins!

B	I	N	G	O

Alternatively, play Blackout Bingo, in which players have to cover their entire card with playing pieces. If you choose to play this type of bingo, make sure your list includes at least 30 titles, names, and details.

You may want to offer small, book-related prizes, such as bookmarks or bookplates.

GR/TD

Book Chain

Create a book chain to link favorite books together. First, cut out strips of colored paper. On one, write down the name of your favorite book. Staple or tape the strip of paper together to form a circle. Now, doing research on the Internet or in encyclopedias, find out about two books your favorite author loved to read as a young person. Write down the title of each book on a strip of colored paper. Staple or tape each strip together, linking the three circles with each other to form a chain.

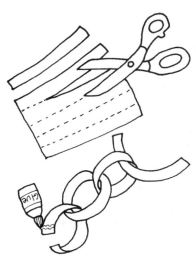

When you are finished reading the books in this chain, research the two new authors on your chain to discover two of their favorite childhood books. Write these titles on colored paper strips and add them to your chain.

In this way, you'll be reading new and interesting books for a long, long time!

Alternatively, you may want to create a chain for each book you read, creating one link for each chapter.

IN/GR

25

Paint a Mural

Do you have a school wall or a playground backboard that could be improved by a brightly-colored mural? First, get permission from authorities to paint the area. Then, choose a scene that illustrates your book. Sketch it out on a large sheet of paper. Talk about color choices and what characters you'll include. Who will paint what part of your mural?

Gather together paints and brushes. You may choose to sketch a design on the wall before painting. Finally, paint a mural to commemorate your book. Remember to wear old clothes and shoes that day! Sign your name at the bottom of your mural so future students will know who painted it.

Alternatively, you might consider mural locations, such as the wall of a local business, an after-school program, or your public library.

GR/TD/SW

Design a Book Jacket

Have you ever heard the phrase, "Don't judge a book by its cover?" We know this to be true. Still, there's no denying that an eye-catching cover compels us to open a book. Design an intriguing cover for your book. It should be different from the publisher's chosen cover, but it should contain the same informational elements.

On the front cover, make sure you include a picture, the book title, author's name, and perhaps a quote from someone in praise of the book. The spine should include the book title, author's name, and publishing house. The spine may or may not include a smaller version of the picture on the front of the book. The back of the book may include a paragraph or two to summarize the book, as well as quotes in praise of the book. Some books include a picture of the author and a short biography on the back cover. Make sure to include the cover illustration and design, the price of the book, and the publisher's name and address on the back cover.

Display your cover to inspire others to read your favorite book!

IN

27

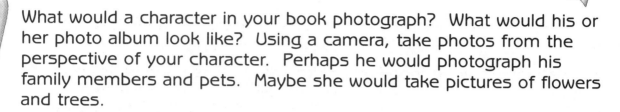

Make a Photo Album

What would a character in your book photograph? What would his or her photo album look like? Using a camera, take photos from the perspective of your character. Perhaps he would photograph his family members and pets. Maybe she would take pictures of flowers and trees.

People using a digital camera can print out their photos. Those using a Polaroid can simply allow their photos to dry, while those using other types of cameras must have their photographs developed.

With your pictures, create your character's photo album. You may choose to purchase an album at the store and arrange the photos under plastic. Or you can create a photo album by taping the photos in a small notebook. Make sure to write the date on which the photograph was taken, as well as the subject of each photograph. Feel free to write further details about the photograph, as well.

IN

Make a Time Capsule

Time capsules are containers that are buried or otherwise hidden and are meant to be discovered many years from now.

Choose your favorite book and write about it. Tell people from the future why this is such a good book. Where can they find the book? What makes this book special and intriguing? What is your favorite part of the book, and who is your favorite character?

Put your writing in an envelope. You may want to include a photo of yourself. Now, seal the envelope. Put it in a plastic bag or other weatherproof container and bury it in a local park or on a playground for someone in the future to discover. (Be sure to get permission ahead of time to dig on public property.)

Alternatively, you may choose to place your time capsule inside a wall that is being built or under a cement slab before it is poured. Whatever you choose, make sure that your capsule is in a place where it will be safe for years.

GR/TD/SW

32

29

Book Garden

What flowers would your characters grow in a garden? What vegetables? Would they plant trees or berries? Would they grow catnip for cats or carrots for horses?

Design a book garden. First, discuss what you'll grow, based on your characters' interests and personalities. Then, nail together a square made of 4' × 1' × 2" untreated planks. Place the square in a sunny area and fill it with garden soil. Divide the plot into 16 square feet.

Now, plant vegetables, flowers, herbs, and fruit. You may choose to label each square with a decorative sign. Perhaps you'll choose to build an even larger classroom garden with stone walkways and a sprinkler system. What would your characters prefer?

GR/TD

A Comic Book

Turn your favorite book into a comic book. Fold at least two sheets of paper in half and staple them so they make a book. With a ruler and pencil, draw boxes across each page to look like blank comic strips. Then, draw the story of your book as if it were a comic. Draw pictures of your characters and have words coming out of their mouths—just as in a real comic strip.

Challenge yourself to make your comic book as funny as possible while staying true to the original story and characters. You may choose to trace over your penciled drawings with black ink and color in your pictures. Don't forget to design a book cover, complete with your name.

When you are finished, trade comic books with your friends and classmates to read and enjoy.

IN

31

Paper Dolls

You can design paper dolls and clothing for the characters in your book. First, gather together pieces of sturdy cardboard and markers, crayons, or colored pencils. Then, draw pictures of the characters. You can keep these pictures fairly simple, focusing mostly on making sure your characters' faces are well-detailed. Outline your doll with black ink, then cut along the outline.

Make a freestanding doll by cutting a ½" slit vertically between your doll's feet and creating a 3" x 2" stand with another vertical slit that fits into the base of your doll. Now, decide what clothing your character will wear. Design it, color it, and cut it out.

Perhaps your character loves beautiful dresses and jewelry. Maybe your character likes to wear overalls and high-top tennis shoes. Make sure your character has at least two changes of clothing. Don't forget appropriate accessories!

Share your paper dolls with friends, and admire the dolls they have created.

IN

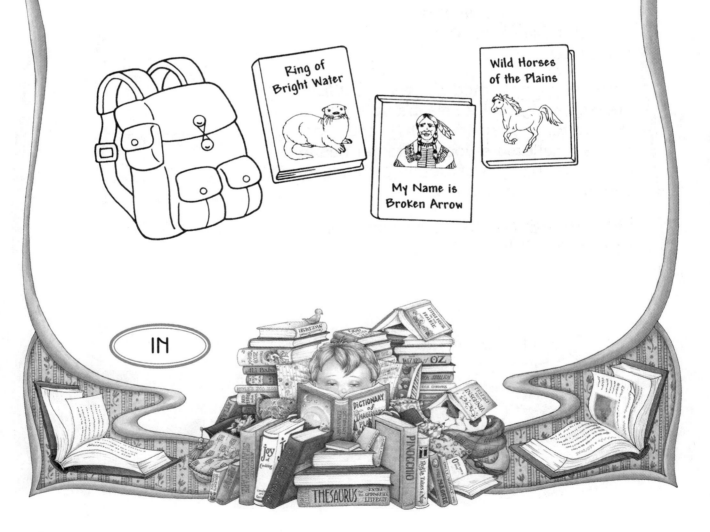

Always Take a Book

Have you ever sat in the doctor's office for an hour with nothing to read except outdated magazines? Maybe you've had to wait with your parents in line at the post office or you've sat in the vet's waiting room for a long time while you waited for your dog to get his yearly checkup. Whatever the case, if you get into the habit of bringing a book with you wherever you go, you'll always have something exciting to do! Train yourself to always take a good book. You might want to carry a small backpack or shoulder bag—something that allows you to carry a book easily from place to place. Don't forget a bookmark!

Ring of
Bright Water

Wild Horses
of the Plains

My Name is
Broken Arrow

IN

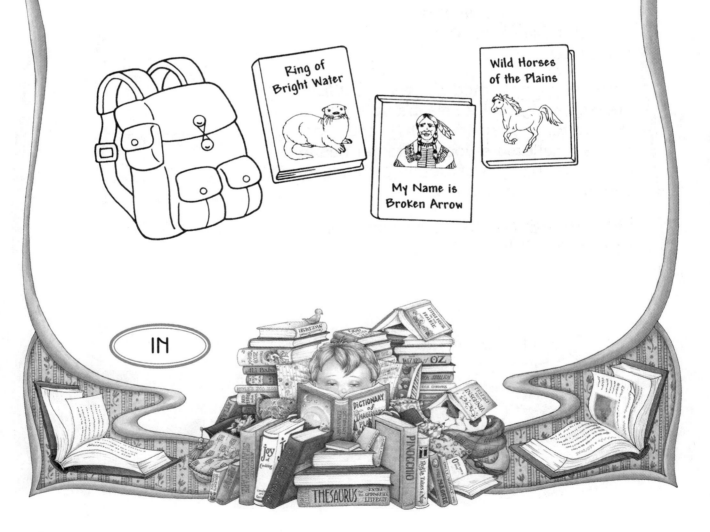

33

Novel Foods

What foods do the characters in your book eat? What do they drink? What are their favorite foods?

Get a better sense of your characters' tastes by cooking their favorite foods. Some characters love sweet things like cookies and ice cream. Other characters like hamburgers and pizza. Decide what foods your characters love. Then, locate appropriate recipes on the Internet or in books and make up a grocery list. Buy groceries and gather necessary materials, such as mixing bowls, spoons, and pans. Cook your characters' favorite foods by yourself or in a group.

Consider sharing your novel foods at a classroom book party or with your family during a special meal!

IN/GR/TD

Give the Gift of Reading

People love to be read to. Many people—especially those who are ill or disabled—benefit a great deal from hearing books read aloud.

Volunteer to read a book at a nursing home, in a hospital, or at a homeless shelter. You might choose to read your favorite book. Alternatively, residents in your chosen location may ask you to read one of their favorites. Remember to read slowly and clearly, showing pictures if your book has them. Pause for questions and discussions about the book, as needed.

Have fun knowing that you have given the gift of reading.

IN/GR/TD

38

35

Host a Book Club

Book clubs are very popular among adults. People read the same book during the month and then get together to discuss it. Sometimes, the host will have a list of specific questions about the book to guide the discussion. Other times, people come to the meeting with questions of their own. Many times, refreshments are served.

You can host a book club, too! Choose one book, and invite people to read and discuss it. Pick a day and time during which you'll all get together. Choose a place, such as someone's living room or a park, and host your book club there. If it is appropriate, consider asking each guest to bring refreshments.

You may want to ask each guest to write down five questions about the book, or perhaps you will supply questions that stimulate conversation about the book. Think about what parts of the book might be confusing. Can other members of the club explain them? Perhaps one member is unclear about part of the plot. Members can help to clarify the book, and increase everyone's enjoyment of it!

Consider holding monthly meetings, in different locations each time. Each member of your book club may have a chance to choose a book, or you may all come up with the month's selection together.

GR/TD

Science Experiment

A good book can inspire a fascinating scientific experiment. First, identify a scientific phenomenon that occurs in your book. Perhaps the main character loves to watch clouds. How are clouds formed? Can you make your own simulated clouds, using information from the Internet or from reference books?

Maybe your characters are involved in a top-secret plan that requires the use of invisible ink. This is easy to make. Simply write your mysterious message with lemon juice and let it dry. Heat the paper with an iron in order to read the secret message!

Do your characters love to grow vegetables? There are many fun and interesting experiments involving vegetables and plants.

Are you interested in finding out how a particular character is able to make paper airplanes that fly perfectly? Why not explore the science involved in this skill and then make your own superior paper airplanes?

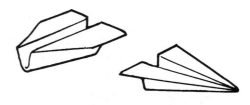

Locate science projects for kids in books at your local library or use an Internet search engine and type in the words "Science Projects for Kids" to find interesting projects. Have fun!

GR/TD

37

Celebrate Reading Day!

Why not choose one day on which to celebrate reading? Plan activities that are all about books and reading. Ask your school principal or a parent if he or she will read a favorite book during lunch. Host a paperback-book exchange or a book raffle. Ask all the students and teachers in your school to vote for their favorite books. Tally the results, then announce them in an assembly.

Use more of the ideas in this book to help make your reading day exciting. Perhaps you'll host a visiting author, make your own books, or read stories to younger children. Be sure to let your local newspapers, radio, and television stations know of your activities three weeks in advance so they can report on your reading celebration. This, in turn, will inspire others to pick up a book!

GR/TD/SW

Design a Website

Websites are easy to design through free programs such as Yahoo! In addition, your Internet provider's server usually allows you to build a web page for free. First, register with a user name and password, and then use the free template to build a website commemorating a favorite book. You may want to invite a knowledgeable parent or community member in to your classroom to assist.

Here are some items to include on your website:

- ❣ the book title and author's name
- ❣ a picture of the book or a graphic element that shows a book and/or pen
- ❣ one paragraph summarizing the book and another explaining why you like this book
- ❣ a picture of the author—and a picture of yourself, as well!

Perhaps you'll want to add links to your page. You can link to an author's official homepage to your school's homepage and to other websites of interest.

Some websites offer a guest book that allows people from all over the world to "sign in" and comment on your site and the book. You may also want to include an e-mail address that allows people to get in contact with you if they want to share an observation or another book discovery!

GR/TD

39

Create a Sand Painting

You can use the technique of sand painting to create a beautiful and lasting tribute to your favorite book. First, draw a scene or character on a piece of heavy paper. Gather several colors of sand (available in craft stores) in different containers. Then, mix together a spoonful of white glue and a spoonful of water. With a paintbrush, paint all areas where you want one color of sand to stick. Sprinkle the sand over the glue and let it sit for a minute. Then, gently turn the paper over and tap it to allow the extra sand to fall off.

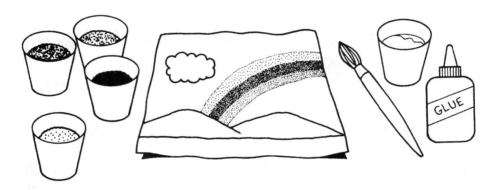

Pour the extra sand back into its proper container. Continue painting glue on your picture and sprinkling different colors of sand on particular areas until your painting is finished. Let it dry on a flat surface, and then display your sand painting for others to enjoy!

IN

Sensory Experience

Good writing appeals to the reader's five senses. Make a chart on butcher paper with five columns. Every time you come across a sensory detail in your book, record it on the chart. For instance, for "Smell," you might write, "cherry blossoms, burnt toast, salt-water." For "Sound," you might write, "cars honking, wind in trees, baby crying."

See	Hear	Taste	Smell	Touch
clouds in the sky	birds chirping	salty air	bacon frying	soft blanket

When you've finished your book and your chart, consider having a sensory celebration. Bring in objects from the book that appeal to your senses. Will you bring in bags of peppermint tea, red roses, or a soft stuffed animal? Maybe you'll bring in a CD by Mozart, a painting by Monet, or green grapes. Whatever you choose, noting the sensory details in your book will help you to remember it forever.

IN

41

Make a Copper Book

In ancient times, people bent and shaped metal in order to make coins, dishes, helmets, and other useful items. You can make a copper cover for a book that summarizes your favorite story.

First, cut a 4" x 7" rectangle out of copper (available at craft and hardware stores). Then, cut out four 4" x 7" pieces of paper. Fold both the copper rectangle and the pieces of paper in half. With a hole punch, punch two half-moon-shaped holes in the fold of your copper rectangle. This will be your book cover. Insert the folded paper into the cover and punch half-moon holes into the paper, just as you did with the copper.

Now, take the pages out of your cover and lay the cover flat on a hard surface. Using a ballpoint pen or sturdy wooden stick, emboss the copper with pictures to illustrate your book. To emboss words or names, write them on a piece of tracing paper, then put it facedown on the back side of your cover. Trace the words or names hard with your ballpoint pen. Then turn the cover over so that the letters are right-side up.

When you are finished embossing your copper cover, write the story of your favorite book on the folded pieces of paper. Illustrate the pages, if you'd like. Then, tie the pages into your book with a piece of string or ribbon.

IN/TD

Stuff Your Characters

You can make simple stuffed characters using sheets of paper and a stapler. Draw your character on a large piece of paper. Place another piece of paper directly behind it, then cut the character out so that you have two shapes that are exactly the same. Color the front and back of your character. Then, staple the two shapes together, leaving the bottom unstapled. You may stuff your character with tissue, newspaper, packing peanuts, or cotton balls. Then, staple the bottom closed. You may want to punch a hole in the top of your stuffed character and hang it on a piece of yarn from the ceiling.

Alternately, you can complete this project using fabric and a needle and thread or a sewing machine. Draw features on your character with permanent ink, or you may choose to appliqué or embroider features onto the material. Stuff your fabric character with cotton batting or another soft material.

Display your characters for everyone to admire!

43

Break the Thermometer!

Set a goal for a number of books to be read by the students in your class or school over several months or during an entire school year. Chart your progress by creating a giant thermometer on paper to be displayed in your classroom or in the school cafeteria. Color the thermometer in with a red marker to show how many books have been read over the months.

If your classroom or school attains its goal, do something extraordinary. Perhaps your class will have a pizza party or go on a special field trip? For example, after one group of students achieved their reading goal, the school principal spent the day on the roof of his school—complete with his desk and telephone!

Alternately, your teachers might promise to put on a talent show, or the entire school may celebrate the achievement of their reading goal with an all-school game day or picnic!

GR/TD/SW

An Author's Life

How much do you know about the author of a favorite book? With just a little research in books, magazines, or on the Internet, you can find out a great deal about an author. Here are some questions to guide you. You might want to display them with the answers on a specially decorated bulletin board.

- What is this author's full name?
- What is this author's date and place of birth?
- What are the names of author's spouse, children, and/or pets?
- What are this author's parents' names?
- What are this author's siblings' names?
- What are this author's favorite books/authors?
- What are this author's hobbies and talents?
- What is this author's favorite subject in school?
- What made this author unique as a child?
- Where did this author grow up?
- Where did this author attend college?
- What other professions has this author worked in?
- Where does this author live now?
- What else has this author written?

IN/GR

45

Create a T-shirt

It's easy to make customized T-shirts to celebrate a favorite book. Simply purchase a light-colored T-shirt and gather together permanent markers or special T-shirt paint.

Draw a design for your T-shirt on a piece of paper. Maybe you'll draw a picture of your favorite character, along with the book title and author's name. Or maybe you'll draw your favorite scene.

When you are finished, place a stack of newspapers inside the shirt, between the front and back. Now, draw or paint on your T-shirt. You may want to decorate both the front and the back—even the sleeves! Allow the ink or paint to dry. Then wear your T-shirt proudly to commemorate your book!

Alternatively, you can design your T-shirt on a computer and purchase an iron-on transfer. Print out your design on the transfer, then iron it onto your shirt.

IN

Book Collage

Think about all the characters, places, and events that make your favorite book such an interesting read. You can create a collage to illustrate this book, using all sorts of fun materials.

First, gather together a large piece of sturdy paper, scissors, and a bottle of glue. Then, locate one or more of the following: fabric scraps, glitter, wrapping paper, buttons, beads, sequins, felt, postage stamps, stickers, old magazines and newspapers, feathers, dried flowers and leaves, ribbon, string, coins, package labels, press-on letters and numbers.

Now, create a vivid and exciting collage to illustrate your book. Think about the characters, settings, and symbols that make your book unique. Cut images out of magazines, or create your own images to depict your particular book. Jumble these images together in crazy shapes and designs.

Your collage should be fun and unusual. When you are finished with yours, display it proudly and explain its significance to friends, classmates, and family members.

47

Local Authors

Coordinate a Local Authors day. Invite local children's authors to your school to read, sell, and sign their books at your school. You can locate local authors on the website for The Society of Children's Book Writers and Illustrators (*www.scbwi.org*) or through your local library. Call local children's authors and invite them to visit your school. (Note that very popular authors often charge money for school visits, and some can only be booked through their publisher; while other authors are happy to visit for free.)

You may want to hold this event in a classroom or an auditorium, depending on how many authors you invite.

Make sure to provide your authors with a podium, a glass of water, and even a microphone, if possible. Assign one person to introduce each author by saying a little about his or her books and why students enjoy them. Allow authors to read from their books and answer questions. Make sure to provide a table on which the authors can display and sign their books.

Don't forget to thank your author with a class-made card and an invitation to enjoy lunch at your school!

GR/TD/SW

Pasta Cars

Pasta comes in all sorts of fun shapes and sizes, in rods and tubes and wheels and spirals. Gather together tubes of white glue and several bags of uncooked pasta in different shapes. Design a pasta car for your characters. Lasagna noodles work well for the base of the car. Penne is good for axles, and round pasta is perfect for your car's wheels!

Take your time and create a truly memorable car for your characters. Make sure to let the glue dry completely, then display your car for others to admire and enjoy.

IN

49

Surround the Room

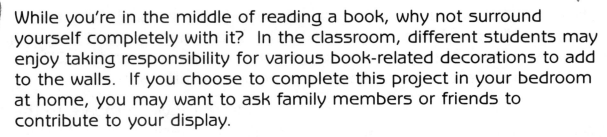

While you're in the middle of reading a book, why not surround yourself completely with it? In the classroom, different students may enjoy taking responsibility for various book-related decorations to add to the walls. If you choose to complete this project in your bedroom at home, you may want to ask family members or friends to contribute to your display.

Perhaps your book has a jungle theme. Using colored paper and staples, create a jungle scene on your walls and ceiling. Don't forget a few monkeys and colorful birds!

Maybe your book takes place by the ocean. Use blue and white tissue paper to create a vivid ocean scene, complete with sharks and whales. A book about outer space can come to life in a room decorated with stars and planets and alien lifeforms!

IN/GR/TD

Watch a Movie

Has one of your favorite books been made into a movie? Why not host a movie day? First, read the book. Then, invite people to watch the film version with you. Gather together a television and a VCR or DVD player. Provide small bags of popcorn and drinks.

After the film, have a discussion. How did the movie compare to the book? What parts were the same? What parts were different? Why might the movie director have changed certain parts of the book? Did the movie characters fit the description of the characters in the book? Which actors did you like the most? Did you like the book or the movie better?

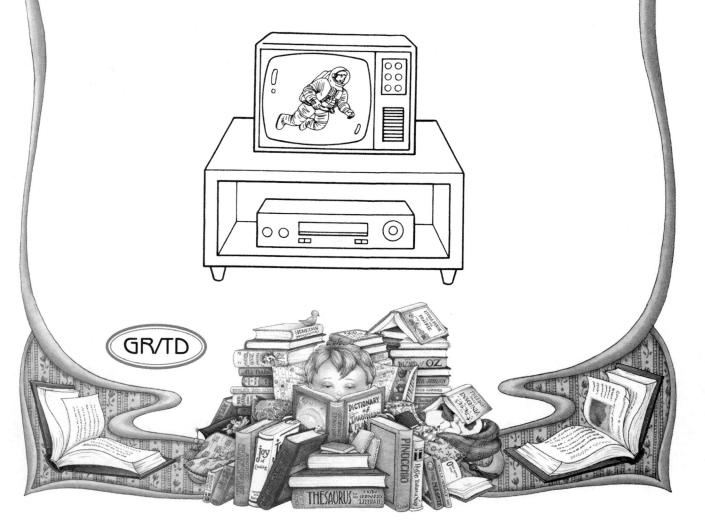

GR/TD

51

Time to Debate

All books have conflicts of some sort. Whether the conflict is between a class bully and a victim, a parent and child, or a dog and a cat, good stories thrive on conflict.

Identify the conflicts in your book. Divide your class in half, forming two teams. Assign each team a position they will take regarding an issue that appears in the book. Give each team at least 10 minutes to gather facts and formulate opinions to support their position.

After both teams have prepared, begin the debate. A teacher or parent can serve as moderator. Allow members of each team to take turns debating the conflict. Try to understand the opposing team's points and address them. Then explain your own points.

Debating the conflicts that appear in books can help you to better understand both the book and the characters!

GR/TD

Papier Mâché Characters

Why not make colorful, long-lasting papier mâché characters to commemorate your book? You'll need balloons or cardboard cartons and tubes of various sizes to create your character. You can tape balloons or cartons together and attach stiff pieces of cardboard for facial features as needed.

After you have designed your character, tear a stack of newspaper into 1" strips. Make a paste of flour and water and dip the newspaper strips in. Plaster the dipped strips onto your balloon and/or cardboard character. Let the first layer of newspaper dry overnight, and then add a second layer.

When the second layer is dry, you can paint your character. Colorful poster paints work well. You might also add sequins, beads, and other decorative items.

You can display your papier mâché character on a shelf or hang it from the ceiling.

IN

56

53

Create a Hall of Fame

High school yearbooks often feature a Hall of Fame—several pages announcing which student was voted the most intelligent, honest, kind, humorous, etc.

Create a Hall of Fame for the characters in your book. Draw a picture of each of them. Below the picture, label the character's "claim to fame." Is your protagonist "Most Heroic"? Is she "Most Attractive"? Maybe one of your favorite characters is "Most Generous," while another is "Most Stingy"!

When you have completed the "Hall of Fame" for each character, display it and discuss it with friends who have read the same book.

Design a Treasure Map

Characters in a book usually want something. Think about what your character really wants. Perhaps it's a new bike or a best friend or first prize for a science project. No matter what your character wants, you can create a treasure map to lead him or her in the right direction.

On a piece of heavy paper, draw a starting point for your character based on the first chapter of your book. You might draw footprints, a road, or stepping stones to mark the path your character will take.

Think about all the obstacles your character has to overcome in the book. Draw these obstacles as landmarks on your treasure map and write clues to help the character make the right decisions.

Does your character get what he or she wants by the end of the book? Draw a picture of the final obstacle this character must overcome, then draw his or her goal inside a treasure chest.

IN

55

Book Trade

Do you have a book that you would love to share with someone? Within your school or community, organize a book trade. Encourage everyone to contribute a favorite paperback book. Ask people to formulate a one-sentence description of the book. Then, walk around and tell people about your book. Listen as they tell you about their book. Trade and enjoy a new book!

For an alternative method of trading, lay out all books on a long table. Allow people to examine each book and to choose one they think they would enjoy.

GR/TD/SW

Character Scrapbook

A scrapbook is a book full of photos, drawings, writing, and mementos designed to help people remember important events. You can make a character scrapbook to commemorate important events and people in your favorite book.

Gather together paper, a hole punch, metal brads or ribbon to bind your book, markers, glue, stickers, and anything else that will make your scrapbook unique. Punch holes in at least three sheets of paper and bind them with ribbon or brads. Then, design your character's scrapbook.

What types of mementos might the character include? Create these and include them in the scrapbook. You might want to include photos or pictures cut from magazines. Stickers are often used to personalize scrapbooks. Sentences or paragraphs interspersed on scrapbook pages help to document important activities, as well as relationships with family and friends.

When you are finished with your scrapbook, display it for everyone to enjoy.

IN

Movie Poster

What if you were allowed to turn your favorite book into a movie? What famous director would direct it? Who would produce it? Which actors would portray which characters? How would the graphics on your poster entice people to come see the movie?

On a piece of large heavy paper, design a poster for the film version of your book. Make sure to choose an exciting picture that ties in with a character or theme from the book. Cast the movie, and list the actors' names on your poster. Don't forget the director and producer. What rating would this movie have? Include it on your poster.

IN

Reading Survey

Conduct a survey to find out which books the people in your community loved as children. Compile an individual list, based on the people below. You might want to share your findings with friends in order to create an even larger list so that you will always have good book recommendations!

As you create your list, don't forget to ask the following people about their three favorite books.

- parents
- teachers
- librarians
- babysitters
- grocery-store cashiers
- doctors
- veterinarians
- camp counselors

- neighbors
- members of your religious community
- bus drivers
- coaches
- aunts and uncles
- grandparents
- cousins
- Anyone else you can think of!

IN/GR/SW

59

Trace Your Book's Illustrations

Tracing can help you to understand more about the illustrations in your favorite book. Using a piece of tracing paper and a good drawing pencil, trace a favorite book cover or illustration. You may want to affix the tracing paper to the book page with paperclips or clothespins so that it doesn't slide around.

Pay attention to the different types of lines used in the picture. Sometimes the artist will use bold, thick lines; other times, he or she will use delicate, fine lines. Think about shading. Where does the artist use shading to create depth and color?

When you are finished with your illustration, write the illustrator's name and the book title at the top. Display your illustration for others to admire.

IN

Interview a Character

Journalists often interview people before writing a magazine or newspaper article. They know that in order to find out interesting details about their subject, they need to ask the "Five W's." These are questions beginning with "Who," "What," "Where," "When," or "Why." They also ask questions beginning with "How."

Pretend you are a journalist writing a story. Choose a character from your book. Write out an interview, including your questions and the character's answers. Then, write an article about the character, based on his or her answers to your questions.

Here are some questions you might ask:

❣ Why do you feel the way you do?

❣ How did you get to where you are at the end of the book?

❣ When did you change during this book?

❣ What do you want out of life?

❣ Who is important to you?

❣ Where do you see yourself in 10 years?

IN

61

Treasure a Book

Why not create a treasure box based on a favorite book? Find a cardboard box. Decorate it with an appliqué technique, gluing overlapping magazine pictures to the cardboard in a collage, and then brushing two layers of white glue over the pictures. (The glue will dry as a clear shellac.)

Now, gather together items that remind you of your book and put them in your treasure box. Does a character love flowers? Why not put a pressed daisy in the box? A foil-wrapped chocolate heart is perfect for a character with a sweet tooth. Think about stuffed animals, framed photographs, coins, stamps, and other objects that you might place in your treasure chest to represent your book.

When you have completed your treasure box, give a brief report on its contents. Be sure to keep your treasure box in a special place to remind you of your favorite book.

IN/GR

Write a Letter

If two characters from your favorite book were to write letters to one another, what would they say? What secrets would they tell? What concerns would they share?

Write a series of letters between two characters. Use different paper and a different writing style for each character so that the letters have an authentic feel. For instance, one character might write in beautiful cursive on pink stationary, sealing the envelopes with rose stickers. Another character might type letters on plain white paper using very formal language. And another character might print in crayon on lined paper, drawing pictures to illustrate important events. The choice is up to you. See if you can create a meaningful dialogue between two characters through letters.

Then display them on a piece of poster board for others to read and enjoy!

IN

Host a Television Talk Show

What if characters from your book appeared on a talk show? What stories might they tell? Would they all get along, or would they argue?

Pretend you are a talk show host. Gather together friends who can portray different characters from your book. Seat them in comfortable chairs and use a microphone in order to interview each character. In your interviews, ask for their different perspectives on events in the book. Also, investigate the characters' relationships to one another.

You might even choose to gather several people to act as a studio audience. Allow people from this audience to ask questions of your characters, as well.

Tape your talk show so that you may show it to friends and family. You may even want to include commercials!

GR/TD

Invite a Guest Reader

Each week, invite a guest reader to visit your classroom or home. The guest might be a parent, grandparent, aunt, uncle, cousin, older sister or brother, community member, political representative, bookstore owner, librarian, or newspaper journalist.

Stories, book chapters, or poems may be selected by the teacher, or by the guest reader. Ask your guest to read for between 15–20 minutes. Allow time for discussion afterwards.

Make sure to thank your guest with a handmade card!

65

Write a Research Paper

Did you discover something in your book that intrigues you? Perhaps the author mentioned hang gliding or scuba diving, raising chinchillas, or exploring Mars.

Using encyclopedias, other books, and/or the Internet, you can write a research paper that will teach you more about the subject of interest.

Try to find at least three published sources about your subject. Take notes, and then write your research paper. Make sure that most of your paper is written in your own words. You may quote from your published sources as needed, citing the author's name and title of the article. Be sure to include a bibliography page at the end of your report to list your sources of information.

Remember that a research report can be exciting. Liven it up with pictures, charts, interviews, and maps. Consider reading it to your classmates or family!

IN

Switch!

What books are your friends reading? In your classroom or at the library, take out the book you are reading. Elect one person to keep time. The timekeeper says, "Go!" Then, everyone reads a book for three minutes. When the timekeeper says "Switch," pass your book to the person on your left and accept a book from the person on your right.

Read for three more minutes, then pass the next book to the person on your left and accept another book from the person on your right. Do this three more times so that you can get an idea of the books that your friends are enjoying.

You may want to write down the titles of books that interest you and make plans to trade books at a later date!

GR/TD

67

Plan a Picnic

What would the characters from your favorite book bring to a picnic? Why not plan an outdoor lunch to celebrate reading? You might assign each guest or group of guests a specific character. Think about what food this character might bring to a picnic. Maybe your character would bring cookies, carrot sticks, or egg-salad sandwiches. Would the character bring sports equipment or an umbrella to protect people from the sun? Perhaps the character would bring a kite or some knitting.

Decide on a location for your picnic, and make up invitations. Don't forget drinks, and blankets or towels to sit on. You may want to come to the picnic dressed as your favorite character. Have fun!

GR/TD

Character for a Day

Choose a favorite character from a book. For an entire day, become that person. First, decide what your character would wear and how he or she would speak and act. How would your character walk? How would he or she eat? Can you pretend to be this person for an entire day?

This can be a classroom activity or even a school-wide activity. Students may prepare three-minute oral reports about their characters to present to the class. Alternately, students may try to guess which character each classmate is portraying.

GR/SW

69

Watercolor Your Book

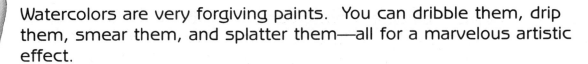

Watercolors are very forgiving paints. You can dribble them, drip them, smear them, and splatter them—all for a marvelous artistic effect.

Think about a scene from your book which would look good depicted in watercolors. Gather together a box of watercolor paints, different-sized brushes, a cup of water, and heavy paper. Now, go wild! Use different brushstrokes to achieve different effects. You may want to shake your wet brush on the page to give the impression of a crashing ocean. Dampen your paper with clean water, and then paint onto it to watch the color spread out like sand. Consider painting some thick lines, some thin lines, and some wiggly lines to add interest to your painting.

When you are finished with your watercolor painting, lay it on a flat surface to dry. Don't forget to sign it in the lower right corner. Make a construction paper frame for your watercolor, then display it for others to enjoy!

IN

Out in the Field

Where might you go in your community to gain a better understanding of the characters and situations in your book? After reading John Steinbeck's *The Red Pony*, you might want to visit a horse stable or farm. Have you just finished *Because of Winn-Dixie*? Why not take a field trip to the local animal shelter, to learn about stray dogs? If you loved *A Single Shard*, you might want to tour your local art museum to see examples of the celadon pottery that the characters make.

Field trips don't have to be expensive, and they can be within walking distance of your school or home. Learning about a new place related to your book can deepen your understanding of the world!

IN/GR/TD

71

Turn Off Your TV!

Each year in April, people around the world celebrate TV Turnoff Week. For at least five days, they pledge not to watch any television. Instead, they spend time outside, learning about the natural world. They do art projects, volunteer to help people and animals in need, and they read!

You can celebrate TV Turnoff Week any time of the year. Choose a week, and organize special events to take the place of time spent in front of the television. Events might include storytelling, acting out a play, reading to younger children, hosting a character picnic or a used book sale . . . the possibilities are endless—and you'll have plenty of time to plan and implement activities since your television won't be on!

Consider using the chart below to record your activities and feelings about TV Turnoff Week.

Day of the Week	Alternative Activity	Observations and Experiences

IN/GR/TD/SW

Keep a Journal

What type of journal would your favorite character keep? Would the character use a waterproof reporter's notebook and scribble almost illegibly about bird-sightings and adventures in the forest? Would your character use flowered paper and write in purple ink about cookies she baked and friends she entertained in her garden?

For a week, keep a journal from the point of view of your favorite character. First, decide what type of book your character would use as a journal, then write your first entry.

What types of events would your character record? What thoughts might he or she write down? For five days, write in your journal as if you were this character.

This assignment makes an excellent alternative to the standard book report, if modified so that journal entries reflect events and people detailed in the book.

IN

73

Books on Tape

People learn best in different ways. Some learn best by reading, some by making things with their hands, and others while walking around the room or running outdoors. Some people learn best by hearing information. Why not record your favorite book on tape so that other people can listen to it?

You'll need a tape recorder, a glass of water, and your favorite book. Find a quiet spot, where there is no background noise. Tape yourself reading, making sure to read slowly and carefully. Feel free to act out characters' individual voices as you read, and make your narration dramatic.

For ideas about how to read, listen to a book on tape from your local library.

You might choose to donate your book on tape to students in a younger grade. Alternately, you might play the tape for blind students or for elderly people who can no longer see well enough to read.

IN/TD

Design a Newsletter

Newsletters are popular among businesses and organizations. They allow employees and members to keep up on current news and learn about people or events in depth.

Design a newsletter for your book. First, study newsletters that you have gathered from community businesses and organizations. Examine the ratio of graphics to text. Notice the layout and the color of paper.

Now, decide what stories you'll include in your own newsletter. Perhaps you'll write an in-depth profile of a character or a description of an important event that occurred in your book. Will you include advertisements? Perhaps you'll add pictures of important characters or events.

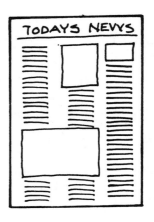

When you have designed your newsletter, decide whether you will create it on the computer or by hand. What color of paper will you use? What additional graphics will you add so that your newsletter is visually exciting? How will this newsletter inform people about your book?

Make copies of your newsletter and distribute it so that people can learn more about your book.

IN/GR

75

Delightful Dialogues

Dialogue refers to conversations between two or more characters. For this exercise in dialogue, you'll need colored paper or posterboard, glue, pens, scissors, and old magazines.

Hello! How are you today?

Cut out two or more pictures of people from magazines and glue them on your paper or posterboard. These people should look roughly like the characters you're portraying.

Create dialogue between the characters, first writing a rough draft on separate paper, then printing a final draft neatly in pen above each cut-out person's head.

Dialogue can reveal a great deal about characters—what they love, what they fear, what they believe in. What will your dialogue reveal about your characters?

IN

Cooking for Characters

What type of meal would your character enjoy most of all? Perhaps he or she has a sweet tooth and would relish a high tea complete with mini-quiches, scones with clotted cream and lemon curd, and petit fours. Maybe your character dreams of going to Italy for pasta, garlic bread, and blackberry gelato.

Create a meal that one of your favorite characters would love to eat. Plan it carefully, making sure that it is both nutritious and delicious.

Come up with recipes and a shopping list. Shop for ingredients, then cook your meal. Serve it in a way that your character would appreciate—on linen tablecloths and fine china, on stumps in the forest, or on TV trays in front of a movie.

The choice is up to you and your character!

IN/GR/TD

Storytime for Pets

Cats and dogs often enjoy being read to. They appreciate the verbal attention—especially if it's accompanied by a loving scratch behind the ears.

Choose your favorite book and read it to a pet. Notice whether he or she particularly likes being read to. Your dog may tilt his head and raise his ears, trying to understand what you are reading. A cat may rub her cheek against you or climb into your lap as you read. You might even want to read a special book about a dog or cat to your pet.

If you do not have a pet at home, consider reading to stray animals at a local shelter. Rabbits, rats, mice, turtles, horses, cows, and even snakes may enjoy being read to, as well! Share your experience in your classroom.

IN

Body Paint!

You can paint your body to look like your favorite character or simply in celebration of a good book. The following body paint is easy to make and easy to wash off.

First, make up a batch of body paint. For each color, stir together the following:

- 1 t. (5 ml) of cornstarch
- ½ t. (2.5 ml) of cold cream (available at beauty and drug stores)
- ½ t. (2.5 ml) of water.

Place globs of this mixture in small containers such as muffin tins or empty yogurt cups.

Add a few drops of food coloring to each glob and blend well.

Now, paint your face, hands, and other parts of your body. You may want to paint your face to resemble that of your favorite character, or paint symbols from your book on your hands and face.

Alternately, paint your friend's face, or set up a face-painting booth at a school book fair or carnival.

IN/GR/TD

79

Crayon Rubbing Illustrations

Crayons can make magical art. For this activity, you'll need a piece of heavy paper, crayons in several colors (including black), and a pair of sharp scissors.

First, cover your paper completely with splotches of different colors—all except for black. Then, color over the top of these colors with your black crayon. Cover the paper completely. Finally, use the edge of a pair of sharp scissors to etch out an interesting scene from your favorite book. As you scrape away the black crayon, the colored crayons will show through, creating an extraordinary picture. Vary the width of your lines, experimenting with thick, thin, and wavy etchings.

You may choose to frame your picture in a simple colored-paper frame and then mount it on a bulletin board or wall.

IN

On Trial

Every book offers some sort of conflict that keeps the story interesting. Organize a court trial to decide the outcome of a conflict in your book. You may first want to watch a trial on television or in person to get an idea of how it is conducted.

Nominate one person to serve as judge and one to be the court reporter. Assign one or more people the role of defending characters and prosecuting characters. Then assign seven people the role of jurors. Don't forget the lawyers, witnesses, specialists, and people watching the proceedings.

Begin the trial in an orderly fashion. The judge and jury should hear testimony from defending characters, prosecuting characters, at her specialists, and witnesses. The court reporter records what everyone has said, and the jury makes its decision about the conflict based on this testimony. The judge hands down the final sentence.

You may choose to videotape your trial to watch later. Discuss how the testimony of various characters resulted in the jury's decision and the judge's sentence.

GR/TD

81

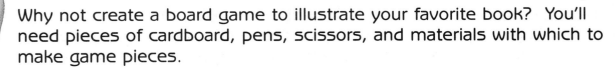

Design a Board Game

Why not create a board game to illustrate your favorite book? You'll need pieces of cardboard, pens, scissors, and materials with which to make game pieces.

First, design your game on a piece of paper. Will you create a path that players must navigate? Some squares on the path might require players to pick a card, move back three spaces, or go to "jail" or another destination based on the story.

Perhaps your game will be three-dimensional, allowing game pieces to slide down chutes and land on teeter-totters that cause a chain reaction of some sort.

However you decide to organize your game, make sure it relates to your book in some manner.

Choose and make game pieces according to symbols or characters in your book. Think about other details, as well. Will you use dice or cards or a pointer that spins? What landmarks from the book might you include on your game board? What conflicts, similar to those in the book, might players have to navigate during the game? What rewards await the winning player?

IN/GR

Soap Sculpture

Michelangelo and Rodin were artists famous for their sculptures. Sometimes sculptors use marble to create timeless art pieces. You can make a lasting sculpture of a favorite character from your book by using a bar of white soap and a butter knife or craft stick.

First, sketch your character on a piece of paper. You might gently trace the image on your bar of soap with a pencil before you begin to sculpt it. When you are satisfied with your sketch, begin to carve out your figure with the knife or craft stick. You can use the end of a pair of scissors to create details such as facial features or fingers and toes.

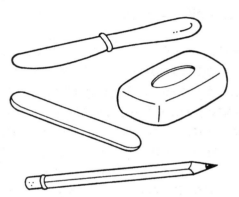

Sculpting takes time and patience. Allow several hours to perfect your sculpture. When it is finished, mount it on a block of wood or a shoebox, then display it in a prominent place for everyone to admire!

IN

83

Film a Documentary

Documentary movies seek to educate people on a certain subject through the use of interviews, video tours, and the filming of key events.

You can write and film a documentary based on an event or topic from your favorite book. All you need is a video camera, a script, and willing actors.

Does your book take place during the Renaissance? You might decide to film a documentary about the plague or about the role of court jesters during this time. Maybe your book centers on the discovery of a rare fossil. Why not recreate an archaeological dig and interview students acting as paleontologists to bring your book to life?

Do the characters in your book love to run? Film a documentary following a day in the life of a runner as he or she prepares for an important race. Interview actors who portray the athlete, coaches, and other runners. Then film the race!

Creating a documentary is an excellent way to gain a greater understanding of the setting, plot, and characters in your favorite book!

IN/GR/TD

Make a Music Video

Music videos rely on both a song and lively images to tell a story. You can make a music video as a tribute to your favorite book.

First, write a song about the book. You may choose to write about one particular character or to tell the whole story in song. Set your song to music. You should have one or more singers, as well as instruments—as many as you wish.

Many times, music videos will include dancing and even scenes acted out in order to better tell a story. You may want to include dancing and acting in your video and costumes that will enhance the performances.

Finally, film your video. Notice the different shots and angles that make your favorite music videos so compelling. Can you use these techniques in your own video?

When you are finished filming your video, show it to an audience.

IN/GR/TD

85

Teacher for an Hour

Give your teacher the day off and volunteer to teach a section of your favorite book for an hour.

You can organize your class in a variety of ways. Perhaps you'll opt to write and administer a quiz on a chapter or two of the book. Later, you can grade the quiz and let students know how they scored.

Alternately, you could lead a classroom discussion, guided by a series of questions about the book. You might choose to go around the room and listen to different students as they talk about their own observations on the chapters or characters or events.

At the end of your teaching session, write a paragraph on what you hoped to teach and what your "students" learned. Describe how it felt to be the teacher for an hour. Would you do it again?

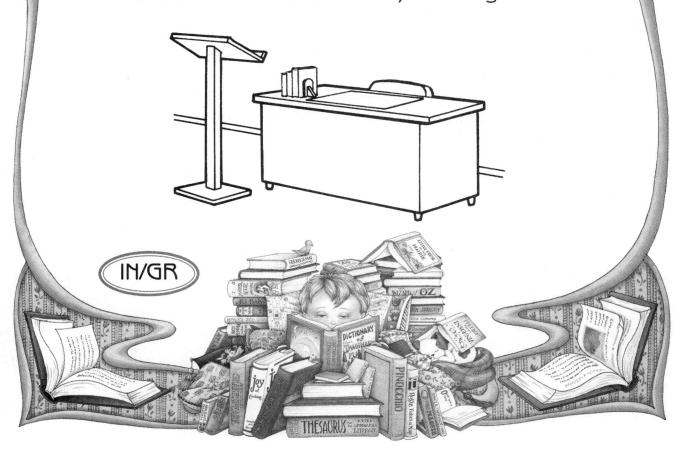

IN/GR

Host a Game Show

You can create a game show to teach people more about your favorite book. Contestants can be asked a series of questions based on several different topics. Possible topics may include "Characters," "Conflicts," "Places," and "Big Changes." Create a large game board on your classroom chalkboard. Award points or small prizes to students individually or in teams.

Another game-show idea is to ask contestants to answer progressively difficult multiple-choice questions and allow them to ask for assistance from friends. You might choose to structure your game show in this way, coming up with easy questions, then more difficult ones about your book. Allow students to ask for assistance in answering questions as needed.

Whatever method you decide on, make sure you assign some students to be contestants and others to be your "studio audience." For additional entertainment, videotape your game show to watch at a later date.

GR/TD

87

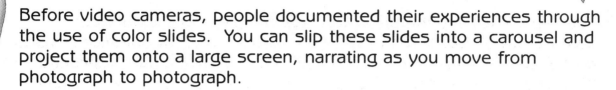

Create a Slide Show

Before video cameras, people documented their experiences through the use of color slides. You can slip these slides into a carousel and project them onto a large screen, narrating as you move from photograph to photograph.

Document your favorite book through color slides. You'll need a camera and color slide film (available at photography stores and some drug stores). What would your characters photograph? What stories would they tell about these photographs?

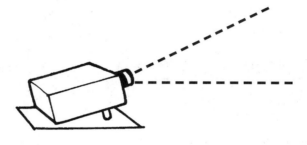

Take your film to be developed and made into slides. Then, using a slide projector and screen, present your slide show. Offer popcorn and juice to your audience. As each image appears on screen, talk briefly about its importance in the book. You may choose to enhance your slide show with music, as well.

Alternately, you may create a slide show using *PowerPoint* on your school computer, projected onto a large screen. Scan photos and create a presentation that you can set to music on the computer.

IN/GR/TD

Clay Figurines

There are many kinds of fun and colorful clay and sculpture compounds available in craft stores. You can create vibrant and long-lasting figurines of your favorite characters with the use of these materials.

First, sketch your character or characters on paper. Decide what colors of clay you will use and how large your characters will be. Then, begin to sculpt. You may choose to make your characters very lifelike or silly and stylized.

Some clay needs to be baked in order to harden; other types dry without additional heat. Check the packaging on your clay to determine drying methods.

You may choose to paint your figurines or leave them unpainted. You can even add accents in the form of dried flowers, sequins, feathers, beads, and anything else you can think of!

IN

89

Write a Zine

Zines are typically low-budget, independently-produced magazines with limited distribution. They can be highly creative, colorful, humorous, deeply honest, and fun! For an up-close look at zines, type the words "zines for kids" into your Internet search engine. National Geographic, Cricket, and other children's publishers offer fun and educational children's zines.

Now, write the story of your book in zine form. First, read several zines (available at local book and music stores, and online) to get an idea of what they are like. Then, come up with text and pictures for your own zine.

How will you tell the story of your book? Will the writing be outrageous and angry? Will it be sweet and wistful? What types of images will you use: photographs, drawings, computer graphics?

Make sure to design a cover for your zine, as well as a masthead identifying the editor, writers, and illustrators.

IN/GR

Make a Quilt

You and your friends can make a colorful quilt to commemorate a favorite book. You'll each need a 12-inch square of fabric. First, plan your square on a piece of paper, thinking about whether you'd like to portray a scene from the book, your favorite character, or symbols from the book. When you've decided what your square will look like, begin decorating your fabric.

You may choose to sew smaller pieces of fabric onto your square or to glue on felt pieces. Think about using buttons, sequins, glitter, and beads to add three-dimensional interest. Alternately, you may choose to decorate your square using fabric-paint (available at craft stores). Put your name on the square, as well. Make sure to include a square that mentions the title of your book and the author.

When all the squares are finished, arrange them to form a quilt and sew them together. For greater durability, you may want to sew another piece of fabric to the back of your quilt.

You can display your quilt by running a wooden dowel through the top hem and then mounting it to a wall.

GR/TD

91

Learn a New Skill

What skills are mentioned in your favorite book? Perhaps a character learns to ride a unicycle. Other characters may create beautiful pottery, learn to juggle, take black-and-white photographs, train dogs, bake layer cakes, or play the guitar.

Identify a skill mentioned in your book. Gather together the materials you'll need to learn this skill. Keep in mind that learning a new skill may take several weeks or months. Commit to practicing this skill at least twice a week. Keep a journal detailing your growing abilities. Finally, organize a talent show to demonstrate your new-found skill!

IN/GR/TD

Create a Classroom Tribute Book

Create a classroom project commemorating a favorite book. Each reader needs a sheet of heavy paper on which to create a tribute to the book. Use markers, crayons, glitter and glue, fabric and felt, beads and buttons, sand, stickers, ribbons, and anything else you can think of to create an exciting page in which you celebrate characters, events, and/or settings from the book.

When you are finished with your page, punch three holes on the left side of it with a hole-punch. Organize all pages into a book, which you may bind with ribbon, yarn, or brads. Instead, you may choose to place your pages in a three-ring binder.

Create a cover for your classroom tribute book and display it at a school open house or other event.

IN/GR

93

Write a Limerick

A *limerick* is a form of humorous poem. Each stanza is five lines long. The first two lines have three feet; they rhyme with the fifth, which also has three feet. The third and fourth lines have only two feet and rhyme with each other.

Limericks typically begin with the words, "There was a . . ." and end with a humorous and unexpected line. Here is an example:

There once was an overfed cat

who hungered to eat a large rat.

He set out some cheese,

But gave a great sneeze,

And fell on his face with a splat!

Write a limerick or two in celebration of your favorite book. Think of a scene or a character that is funny and commemorate it in verse!

You may choose to print your limerick on attractive paper with a border, then display it on a bulletin board or in a classroom book. Alternately, you may want to have a public reading of your limericks so that everyone may enjoy them.

IN

Hold a Poetry Slam

Poetry slams feature poets reading their work in an energetic performance, then receiving Olympic-style judging from a panel, to which an audience responds.

Individually or in groups, write a performance poem based on a book. Use exciting language and imagery. Then practice reciting your poem out loud so that it is dramatic and interesting.

When you are ready, organize a poetry slam. Assign four people to act as judges. They should have large sheets of paper and markers with which to write down scores. Individually or in groups, perform your poem. Allow the audience to cheer you on as you perform. The judges should then write down a score and hold it up on their paper. The audience should react accordingly.

The goal of a poetry slam is to celebrate language in a fun and friendly competition. Award all participants a prize in the form of a certificate or treat.

IN/GR/TD

Make a Mask

Masks can be beautiful and lasting ways to commemorate a book. Choose a character from your favorite book. Sketch out a design for your mask, planning size and shape, as well as facial features.

Now, decide how you'll make your mask. Papier mâché over a balloon the size and shape of your head can be dried, and then cut in half lengthwise for a mask. You may choose to papier mâché or decoupage boxes or other cardboard structures. Craft stores sell strips of plaster which adhere to your face when dampened and then form a cast that can be decorated. Make sure to put petroleum jelly on your face before adhering plaster strips, and avoid the eye and mouth areas.

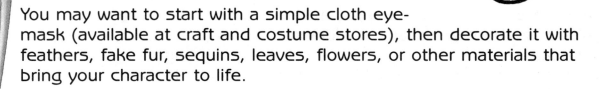

You may want to start with a simple cloth eye-mask (available at craft and costume stores), then decorate it with feathers, fake fur, sequins, leaves, flowers, or other materials that bring your character to life.

When your mask is completed, stage a parade or other celebrations to show off your work, and rejoice in your favorite book!

IN/GR

Perform a Melodrama

Melodrama is a form of theater in which audiences are encouraged to applaud the good characters and boo the villains. They may also sing along with the characters on stage, and laugh at their humorous antics, as well as warn characters of possible danger.

Rewrite your book as a melodrama. Make sure you have clearly described good characters and bad characters. Often, melodrama will put good characters into dangerous situations. For example, villains tie people to railroad tracks as a train approaches, or bind them to chairs, or lock them in closets. Create humorous situations, giving the audience a chance to both laugh and to warn characters of danger. In classic melodrama, the good characters are rewarded, while the villains are punished.

When you have written your melodrama, rehearse it until you are ready to perform. Often, a pianist or other musicians provided accompaniment to classic melodrama. Do you have such a musician in your group?

You might choose to serve your audience popcorn and other refreshments as they actively participate in your exciting melodrama with cheers, hisses, boos, warnings, and lots of laughter!

GR/TD

Make Hieroglyphs

The writing system used in ancient Egypt, called hieroglyphs, consisted of small pictures. It was also used as an alphabet.

You can make modern-day hieroglyphs using symbols and ideas from your favorite book. You'll need a piece of paper and a pen, pencil, or paints and a paintbrush. First, list the alphabet with plenty of space after each letter for your picture. Now, think about what symbols would best represent your book. For example, in a book about dogs, you might choose to represent the letter B with a picture of a bone, the letter C with the picture of a collar, and the letter D with a picture of a dog. In a book about the ocean, you might choose to draw an anemone for the letter A, a beach ball for the letter B, and a crab for the letter C.

Draw a picture after each letter. Then, write a paragraph describing your book using your hieroglyphs. Pass the paragraph, along with your new alphabet, to a friend to decode.

Create Stained-
Glass Pictures

Stained glass has been around for centuries. You can use markers and a piece of tracing paper to make a pretend stained-glass picture to hang in a window.

First, sketch a picture inspired by your book on a piece of scrap paper. Then, draw the picture with a thick black marker on your tracing paper. Make sure to add details of the kind you would find in stained glass windows, such as feathers on a bird's wing, waves on the ocean, or leaves on a tree.

Finally, color your picture with markers. Frame it in a colored-paper frame. Hang the picture in a window, allowing the sun to illuminate your artwork.

99

Design a Coat of Arms

In the days of King Arthur, knights identified themselves in battle by showing designs on their shield. You can create a coat of arms for a character or characters in your book. You'll need colored paper, markers, glue, old magazines, stickers, glitter, and any other craft supplies you'd prefer.

First, copy the coat of arms and banner on page 109. Then, design your coat of arms according to your character's interests and beliefs. Think about what colors and symbols your character would prefer. You may choose to divide your coat of arms into sections in order to clearly display your character's identifying marks.

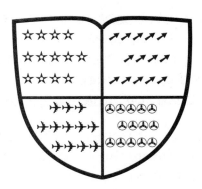

Finally, think of a motto for your character. Write it on the banner below your coat of arms. Display your work on a bulletin board or wall and explain the significance of each symbol and color to friends, classmates, and family members.

IN

Make a Puzzle

Choose a scene from your favorite book. Draw it in bright colors on a piece of stiff cardboard. Using a black marker, draw puzzle pieces on top of the picture. On the other side, write a paragraph about the scene, explaining the setting and characters, as well as the action depicted.

Also, think about whether you want to photocopy your puzzle in order to give people a good model of what your picture will look like when the puzzle is completed.

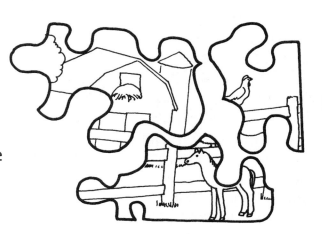

Now, carefully cut out your puzzle pieces. You may choose to laminate your puzzle pieces at this point for greater durability. After lamination, cut your pieces out once more.

Finally, put them in a box or in an envelope with your photocopied picture. Give them to a friend to put together and enjoy. This project makes a wonderful gift for younger students who are just learning to read and put together puzzles.

101

Soap-on-a-Rope Characters

You can create fun and useful soap characters to give as gifts or use yourself.

First, cut a piece of yarn long enough to fit around your neck and tie the ends in a knot. Now, prepare a batch of soap-dough by grating a bar of soap into a bowl. Mix two cups (500 ml) of these soap flakes with ½ cup (125 ml) of water and a few drops of food coloring. Beat this mixture, then press it into a firm glob and press it onto the yarn just above the knot. Squeeze it tightly so that it won't fall off.

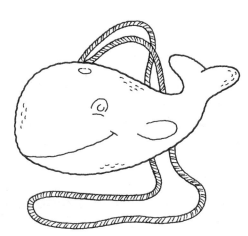

Now, shape the dough into your favorite book character. Let the soap dry for a few days, then tie another knot in the yarn right where it comes back out of the soap. Wrap your gift in special paper and present it to the recipient, or use the soap yourself.

IN

Parent Certificate of Achievement

This is to certify that

_____

parent of

_____

made a difference in the life of a reader.

This parent, through time and attention to books,
taught a child that reading is both fun and important.

Thank you for helping to create a lifetime reader!

_____   _____
Teacher   Date

Student Certificate of Achievement

This is to certify that _____,

student in Room _____,

read a book to _____,

student in Room _____,

and made a difference in the life of a reader.

This student gave time and energy in order to teach a child about the importance of reading good books.

Thank you for helping to create a lifetime reader!

_____   _____
                Teacher   Date

STAR
READER!

_____

_____

Student Name:

_____

_____

_____

Book Title

Coat of Arms and Banner

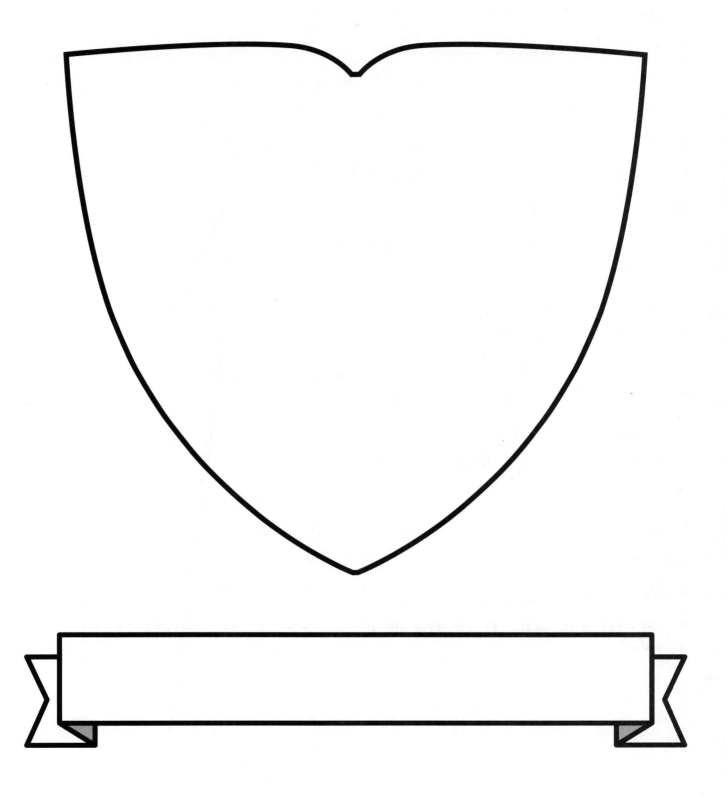

109

Character Profile

Use this profile to explore a character from your favorite book. Get into the mind of the character, then fill in the blanks.

Book _____

Author _____

Character's Name _____

Age: _____ Height: _____ Weight: _____

Male/Female: _____ Hair Color: _____ Eye Color: _____

Where does this character live? _____

_____

Who is this character's best friend? _____

_____

Who are this character's enemies? _____

_____

What are this character's plans for the future? _____

_____

Fill in the blanks to describe this character further.

Favorite Color: _____ Favorite Food: _____

Favorite Animal: _____ Favorite Hobby: _____

Favorite Sport: _____ Favorite Music: _____

Favorite Place: _____ Favorite Movie: _____

Would you like to be this character's friend? Why/why not? Explain in the space below.

List of Books and Authors

Directions: Fill this list out as you finish reading each book this year.

Date	Title	Author	My Feelings about this Book

Especially for Parents!

Ways to Inspire a Love of Reading

❣ Read books, magazines, and newspapers around your child. Show your child that you love to read. Read interesting excerpts aloud to your child during mealtimes, or in the evening. Discuss ideas and opinions with your child in a comfortable, non-judgmental setting.

❣ Read aloud regularly to your child. Establish a daily storytime with favorite books that your child has chosen. Make this time fun and interesting. Encourage your child to ask questions and discuss the books you read. Make your voice enthusiastic as you read, and don't be afraid to portray different characters by using different voices. Children love this!

❣ Encourage your child to read by providing a well-lit area with bookshelves full of books and magazines that your child has helped select. Establish a regular reading routine and keep a record of books read that your child can add to and appreciate. Consider offering an incentive for books finished. (A sticker, a penny, or other reward works well.)

❣ Limit your child's exposure to television, movies, and video games. Offer fun alternatives—not only good books and magazines, but interesting art and science projects, puzzles, and trips to the library, museums, zoos, and local historical sites.

❣ Keep in touch with your child's teacher. Find out what your child is reading at school and discuss the books at home. Ask the teacher how you may help in or out of the classroom. Consider volunteering to read in the classroom, or do a show and tell presentation related to a classroom book.

❣ Teach your child how to care for books. Discuss the importance of keeping books clean so that others may enjoy them. If they are treated with respect, books will last for hundreds of years. Share some of your well-cared-for childhood books with your child.